For Your Summertime Enjoyment

This summer, we're serving up something special for HFCplus customers like you. This cookbook is packed full of your favorite barbecue recipes.

Wherever you live, whatever your favorite dishes, you're sure to find something that delights both family and friends in the following pages.

One More Way We're Working For You

Editor: Jane Doyle Guthrie

ISBN 0-925175-17-X

Printed in the United States of America

10 9 8 7 6 5   9 8   9 9

Pig Out Publications, Inc.
4245 Walnut
Kansas City, MO 64111
(816) 531-3119

CONTENTS

★ ★ ★ ★ **ACKNOWLEDGMENTS** ★ ★ ★ ★

Charles Custer/Boss Pit, for Custer's Eola Hotel Pickled Vidalia Onions;

Ed Daniels/Quality Hogs, for Big Ed's Pork Steaks and Big Ed's Barbecued Catfish Fillets;

Darrell Hicks/Cajun Country Cookers, for Cajun Beef Sausage, Spicy Cajun Chicken Breasts, and Cajun Tuna;

Jim Marty/Hogaholics, for Hogaholics Award-Winning Ribs and Hogaholics Dry Rub, Basting Sauce, and Wet Sauce;

Bubba Norris/Pork Forkers, for Uncle Beaver's Marinated Duck Breasts;

Jim Quessenberry/Arkansas Trav'lers, for Country Boy Pork Tenderloin, Quessenberry's Prime Rib, Trav'lers Turkey Oregano, and Spiced Ginger Shrimp;

Jerry Roach/J-R's Cook'n' Crew, for Smoked Pork Chops, Spicy Smoked Roast Beef, J-R's Smoked Chicken, Prawns in Lemon Butter, Smoker-Cooked Beans, and J-R's Basting Sauce;

Bill Thompson/Paddlewheel Porkers, for Melt in Your Mouth Steak;

John Thompson/Paddlewheel Porkers, for Lemon Grilled Orange Roughy;

Jim Turner/Super Swine Sizzlers, for Sizzlers Pork Shoulder and Super Swine Sizzlers Dry Rub, Basting Sauce, and Barbecue Sauce;

John Willingham/Willingham's River City Rooters, for W'ham Wings.

BARBECUE BASICS

It doesn't take a Ph.B. to appreciate the not-too-subtle difference between barbecuing and grilling. When you're grilling, the fire's *hot*. Meats cook rapidly over direct heat to maximize juice retention and seal in moisture. Barbecuing, on the other hand, involves *slow* cooking, at a relatively low temperature (180 to 300 degrees), over either direct or indirect heat. Both methods, of course, have merit. Whether you're grilling or barbecuing/smoking, though, the basic equipment stays essentially the same.

Equipment

When deciding on your "rig," there are lots of options:

The *open brazier* is a shallow container with a grid on which to put what you're cooking (like a hibachi); it's suitable only for grilling.

Covered cookers come in all shapes and sizes, from Weber-type "kettles" to rectangular units. They serve for both grilling and barbecuing. To use for barbecuing, the unit must have vents for proper ventilation and temperature control.

The *Japanese kamado* is a ceramic "egg-shaped" cooker, with a firebox in the bottom and an adjustable air vent. The tight-fitting lid makes it an excellent smoker.

A *water smoker* is a dome-shaped cooker with a firebox in the bottom, a water tray in the middle, and a grid at the top. It's excellent for slow smoking with indirect heat.

Gas or electric grills are easy to use and clean and are popular with weekend chefs. Primarily for grilling, they can be used to barbecue by keeping the heat very low and adding a water pan for moisture. Smoke flavor can be

achieved by wrapping wood chips in heavy-duty aluminum foil, poking holes in the packet, and then placing it
directly on the lava rock. When you're through cooking,
you discard the smoke chip packet. No mess, great smoke
flavor.

A *55-gallon drum* can make a great cooker. Your
neighborhood pitmaster or a more comprehensive book on
barbecue can show you how to build your own.

Tools and Accessories

After deciding on your cooker, there's a basic reper-
toire of tools to put together:

The *meat thermometer* is the most under-utilized
utensil in barbecue cookery. Use it to measure the internal
temperature of your meat to check for doneness.

A *charcoal chimney* offers a clean, handy way to start
charcoal. Load the chimney with charcoal and newspaper,
and you can start a fire without petroleum or chemical
products.

Use two pairs of *tongs*—one for handling meats (never
pierce meat with a fork) and the other for moving or refuel-
ing hot coals.

Keep a *spray bottle of water* handy to extinguish flare-
ups.

A *heavy-duty glove, mitt, or hot pad* is a must to pro-
tect your hands.

Either a *basting brush, paint brush, or small cotton
"mop"* will do a great job for basting.

Place a *candy thermometer* in the top vent of your
grill to gauge your cooking temperature.

Invest in a sturdy *wire brush* to keep your grill clean.

Never appear grill-side without a *snazzy apron*. How
else will they know you're the Chief Chef?

Fuel

Always use high quality hardwood charcoal briquettes or lump charcoal (cheaper varieties can contain a great deal of coal). You can start your coals either in a chimney starter or right in the cooker. To do so, make a mound of briquettes and douse them with charcoal starter before lighting (*never* use gasoline). Allow briquettes to burn until they are 80% ashed over. Spread them out, replace the grill, and you're ready to cook.

Wood chips or chunks will add to the smoke flavor, and most non-resinous woods work well. Pieces can be soaked first in water and then placed directly on the coals. As an alternative, wrap the chips (wet or dry) in heavy-duty aluminum foil, poke holes in the top of the packet, and place the bundle right on the coals.

Most people are familiar with barbecued foods smoked in hickory or mesquite, and both are widely available. However, fruitwoods are wonderful for smoking—apple, cherry, peach, pear. Grapevine adds a light delicate taste to fish or chicken. Pecan, alder, sassafras, or persimmon also add flavor and aroma. By all means experiment; just don't use pine!

Moisture

Some swear that a water tray is a necessary element of good barbecue cookery; others never use one. Try it both ways and decide for yourself. The water tray or pan can be placed directly on the coals to create indirect heat, or it can be placed to one side of the grill. Either way, it imparts moisture in the cooking chamber.

Rubs, Marinades, and Sauces

Barbecue cooking is a subjective experience, and that's why this book offers such a variety of sauces, rubs, and marinades. Many teams are devoted to particular brands when concocting their signature "tastes," and you'll see this reflected in their recipes. If a brand name is specified that's not available in your area, substitute your favorite (or check the "Mail Order Sources" at the back of this book). Be creative and use your favorite herbs and spices for recipe variations.

Rubs are blends of dry spices. Dry rubs are applied to the meat to tenderize and flavor it prior to cooking.

Marinades are liquid blends in which meats soak prior to cooking. Some can also be used as bastes during the cooking process. Marinades contain spices, vinegar, wine, and/or other flavorings as well as tenderizing agents that are absorbed into the meat.

Sauces are generally tomato-based blends that can enhance your barbecue. They should be used only during the final stages of cooking or served "on the side" as a condiment.

Time

Grilled meat and side dishes can be completed in relatively short order, but barbecuing "takes as long as it takes." Cooking times will vary with the type of cooking unit, the amount of fuel, and the size of the cut of meat. So, relax, get out your handy meat thermometer, and follow the directions that come with it. Beef and lamb are rare at 130 degrees and well done at 160 degrees. Pork should be cooked to 170 degrees, and poultry to 165 degrees.

Good luck!

★ ★

PORK

★ ★

Award-Winning Barbecue Ribs

2 slabs pork ribs

DRY RUB MIX:

1 T. lemon peel
1 T. garlic powder
1 T. onion powder
1 T. chili powder
1 T. paprika
1 T. MSG (optional)
1/2 black pepper
1/2 T. cayenne pepper
1/2 T. white pepper
2 T. salt
2 T. sugar

BASTING SAUCE MIX:

4 C. Wicker's Barbecue Marinade and Baste
2 C. vegetable oil
2 C. apple cider vinegar
1/2 C. lemon juice

Skin ribs and set aside for 1 hour to reach room temperature.

Combine Dry Rub Mix ingredients and rub into both sides of ribs. Place meat on grill away from coals, bone side down. Combine Basting Sauce ingredients. Cook ribs 1-1/2 to 2 hours, never turning, before using basting sauce. Cook slowly for 3-1/2 to 4-1/2 hours, basting every 45 minutes to 1 hour. Serve with barbecue sauce on the side, or (not recommended by purists) baste with barbecue sauce the last 1/2 hour.

Serves 4-6

Famous Loin Back Ribs

2 slabs baby back ribs
warmed honey

DRY RUB MIX:

3 T. paprika
1 T. onion powder
1 T. garlic powder
1 T. ground basil
1-1/2 T. dry mustard powder
1 T. red pepper
1/2 T. black pepper

    Combine dry rub ingredients and rub onto ribs. Cook ribs over hickory coals at 190-200 degrees for 4 to 5 hours. 15 minutes before serving, coat the ribs with heated honey.

Serves 4-6

Barbecued Baby Back Ribs

2 (2 lb.) racks baby back ribs
Holy Smoker, Too Sprinkle Spice (p. 45)
prepared mustard

Sprinkle spice *liberally* over ribs and then coat with prepared mustard. Place in a plastic storage bag in refrigerator overnight.

Cook at 275 to 300 degrees for approximately 5 hours over hickory charcoal and water-soaked hickory chips to produce hickory-smoked flavor.

Serves 4-6

Smoked Pork Chops

6 pork chops (1-1/2 to 2-in. thick)
salt and pepper to taste
dry barbecue seasoning mix (optional)
Kraft Thick 'n Spicy Barbeque Sauce

Heat grill to about 225 degrees. Season chops with salt and pepper or with dry barbecue mix (commercial or make your own).

Place chops in center portion of grill, maintaining a slow temperature of 225 to 250 degrees. Cook for 2 hours, turning once. Use barbecue sauce to finish meat the last 15 to 20 minutes or serve on the side.

Serves 6

Country Boy Pork Tenderloin

3 large pork tenderloins

MARINADE:

1-1/2 C. apple butter
1 C. white vinegar
2-1/2 T. Worcestershire sauce
2 T. brandy
1 T. soy sauce
1 T. sugar
1 t. dry mustard
1 t. salt
1/2 t. pepper
1/2 t. paprika
dash of Tabasco sauce

Combine marinade ingredients, blend well, and pour over tenderloins. Marinate at least 2 hours, preferably overnight.

Barbecue loins for about 3 hours over semi-direct charcoal fire, turning and basting with marinade approximately every 30 minutes until done.

Serves 6-8

Big Ed's Pork Steaks

6 pork steaks
K.C. Masterpiece Barbecue Sauce (or your choice)
1 T. garlic salt
Rendezvous spice

DRY SPICE MIX:

1 part garlic powder
1 part McCormick Barbecue Spice
1/2 part celery salt
1/8 part hickory-flavored salt

Combine Dry Spice Mix ingredients and rub into pork steaks. Refrigerate meat overnight.

Grill steaks over charcoal for 30 to 45 minutes at 250 degrees. Baste with barbecue sauce, and sprinkle lightly with garlic salt and Rendezvous spice. Use a basting brush to work garlic salt and Rendezvous spice into the sauce. Cook 30 more minutes and serve.

Serves 6

Sizzlers Pork Shoulder

1 pork shoulder

DRY POWDER MIX:

2 t. paprika
1 T. onion salt
1 T. garlic salt
1 T. ground basil
1-1/2 T. lemon pepper
1 T. red pepper
1-1/2 T. black pepper
1 T. mustard flour

BASTING SAUCE (optional):

1/2 gal. vinegar
1 qt. Super Swine Sizzlers Barbecue Sauce (p. 50)
8 oz. Super Swine Sizzlers Dry Powder Mix (recipe above)

Preheat cooker to 250 degrees. Trim all excess fat from shoulder; combine Dry Powder Mix ingredients and rub into meat. Prepare a batch of Basting Sauce if desired.

Put meat on grill. Place a small stick of green hickory wood beside briquettes for more smoke, as desired. Keep heat between 250 and 300 degrees for first 6 to 8 hours, then reduce heat and maintain at 250 degrees for remainder of time. If basting, do so about every 3 hours. Cook 20 to 24 hours total time. Shoulder is done when internal temperature reaches 170 degrees.

"Pull" meat into pieces with a fork or tongs, then separate out the more charred pieces and chop to mix back in. Pile on buns and enjoy!

Serves several

Volunteer Fire Department Whole Roasted Hog

135-150 lb. hog
olive oil
butter
seasonings to taste (mixture of red and black pepper, garlic,
    lemon pepper, oregano, thyme, onion, salt, etc.)
marinade (your choice)

Rub hog's skin with olive oil and the cavity with butter and seasonings. Place on cooker skin-side up for first 4 to 5 hours, keeping skin moist by spraying with olive oil as needed. Turn hog and fill cavity with additional seasoning and marinade of choice. Cook for another 14 to 16 hours.

Serves at least 75

★ ★

BEEF

★ ★

Barbequed Beef Tenderloin

3-4 lb. beef tenderloin

MARINADE:

1/2 C. red wine
1/2 C. soy sauce
2 T. sesame oil
2 T. honey
2 cloves garlic, minced
1 T. ground ginger

Trim fat from tenderloin and bring to room temperature. Combine marinade ingredients and place with tenderloin in a sealable plastic bag. Refrigerate overnight.

Remove from marinade and cook over low fire with grill covered. Cook for 1 to 1-1/2 hours, basting and turning every 15 minutes.

Serves 6-8

Spicy Smoked Roast Beef

1 well-marbled chuck roast, room temperature
salt and pepper to taste
1/2 C. J-R's Basting Sauce (p. 48)
1/2 C. Kraft Thick 'n Spicy Barbeque Sauce with Honey
1/2-3/4 C. broth (reserved from roast)

Sprinkle roast with salt and pepper, and wrap tightly in heavy-duty foil. Place toward hotter end of smoker and cook about 4-1/2 hours, maintaining a temperature of about 225 to 250 degrees. Uncover and check for tenderness.

Pour accumulated broth off roast and mix with basting sauce and barbecue sauce. Make a pan under the roast from the foil and pour over the meat. Leave uncovered, making sure that water level in the smoker is sufficient to keep the meat from drying out, and close the top damper almost completely. Keep meat moist and let the flavor soak in.

Serves 6-8

Melt in Your Mouth Sirloin Steak

2 (3 lb.) sirloin steaks (1-1/4 to 2-in. thick)

MARINADE:

1/3 C. Worcestershire sauce
1-1/2 t. granulated garlic
1-1/2 t. lemon pepper

Coat steak with Worcestershire sauce and rub in dry marinade seasonings with fingers (amounts listed are approximate; be sure both sides are thoroughly coated). Refrigerate marinated meat for 2 hours prior to cooking.

Sear for 2 minutes on each side on hot grill. Reduce heat to medium to low, cook to taste (rare, 4 minutes each side; medium, 6 minutes each side; well, 8 minutes or longer each side).

Serves 6-8

Cajun Beef Sausage

1/2 lb. ground beef
1 T. Cajun Country Seasoning

Mix ground beef with cajun seasoning. Blend well and make into small patties. Grill over medium heat until brown.

Great breakfast sausage!

Serves 4

Garlic Grilled Flank Steak

1-1/2 lb. flank steak, trimmed
3-4 cloves garlic, minced
3/4 C. Italian dressing
1/4 C. red wine

Mix all ingredients in a sealable plastic bag. Marinate steak in refrigerator overnight.

Sear meat over hot coals for 5 minutes per side for rare meat (longer to taste, but do not overcook). To serve, slice meat on the diagonal across the grain.

Serves 4

Quessenberry's Prime Rib

15-16 lb. standing rib roast, nicely marbled
1 t. garlic powder
1/4 C. olive oil
freshly cracked black peppercorns
horseradish sauce (optional)

With a boning knife, carefully separate the rib bone from the roast, keeping in one piece. Remove the "lip" or fat layer in one piece. Sprinkle the ribeye with garlic powder, then reassemble the pieces. Tie with butcher's string, binding at each rib. Brush generously on all sides with olive oil and cover entire surface with cracked pepper.

Cook on a closed grill over medium (250-degree) indirect heat. Cook for 2 to 3 hours, until internal temperature reaches 140 degrees (medium rare). Wrap roast tightly in foil to allow a little extra steaming time. Remove foil, carve into 1/2-inch thick slices; the outside will be well done and the center rare. May be served with horseradish sauce.

Serves a bundle

Beef Kabobs

2 lbs. beef, cut into 1-in. cubes
1 tomato, cubed
1 onion, cubed
1 green pepper, cubed
8 whole mushrooms

MARINADE:

1/2 C. red wine
2 T. olive oil
2 T. honey
1 clove garlic, minced

Combine marinade ingredients, add cubed beef, and refrigerate for 2 to 3 hours.

Remove meat from marinade and thread onto skewers, alternating with vegetables. Grill over medium-hot coals for approximately 12 to 15 minutes, turning and basting often with marinade.

This is a very simple, colorful entree, delicious served over a bed of rice.

Serves 4

Perfect Strip Steaks

4 New York strip steaks
4 T. olive oil

SPICE RUB MIX:

1 T. garlic salt
1 T. paprika
2 t. basil
2 t. oregano
1/2 T. black pepper
1 t. cayenne pepper

Combine Spice Rub Mix ingredients. Lightly coat steaks with oil, then rub in spice mix until well coated. Let stand at room temperature for 1 hour, then grill over hot coals for 4 to 6 minutes each side.

Serves 4

★ ★

POULTRY
AND GAMEBIRDS

★ ★

Trav'lers Turkey Oregano

2 turkey breasts

MARINADE:

1 C. lemon juice
4 C. olive oil
2 t. salt
1 t. garlic powder
1 T. dried oregano

Place breasts in a glass dish. Combine marinade ingredients and pour over meat. Cover and refrigerate for several hours.

Remove turkey from marinade; cook over 200- to 225-degree coals in a covered grill for 20 to 30 minutes per pound. Turn and baste with reserved marinade every 20 to 30 minutes, basting with reserved marinade until done.

Serves 10-12

J-R's Smoked Chicken

3 chicken fryers, quartered or halved
salt and pepper to taste
Kraft Thick 'n Spicy Barbeque Sauce

Preheat smoker to approximately 250 degrees. Sprinkle salt and pepper on fryer pieces and place on cooker, bone-side down. Maintain temperature level and cook 1-1/2 hours. Start basting chicken with barbecue sauce during the last 30 minutes. Leg bone will twist easily when the chicken is done.

Serves 6-8

Spicy Cajun Chicken Breasts

4 (6 oz.) boneless and skinless chicken breasts
Italian dressing
Cajun Country Seasoning

Marinate chicken in Italian dressing for 24 hours. Remove from marinade and sprinkle lightly with Cajun Country Seasoning. Grill over medium fire for 15 minutes.

Makes delicious sandwiches, may be sliced and added to a salad, or can be served whole as main dish.

Serves 4

David Cox's Marinated Chicken

2-3 lb. chicken
1 stick margarine
1 C. brown sugar
1/2 C. soy sauce
1/2 C. red wine
2 t. dry mustard
1/2 t. garlic salt
1/2 t. black pepper
1/4 C. lemon juice

In a saucepan, combine butter with liquids and spices, and boil for 5 minutes. Pour mixture over chicken and refrigerate for 24 hours.

Place chicken in a smoker and cook for 200 to 225 degrees for about 2 hours until done.

Serves 3-4

W'ham Wings

3 lbs. chicken wings (drummie and second bone)
W'ham Seasoning (Mild or Cajun Hot)
W'ham Barbecue Sauce
bleu cheese dressing

Heat grill to medium-hot (400 to 450 degrees). Put chicken and W'ham Seasoning in a plastic bag; shake to coat chicken pieces. Allow to marinate at least 20 minutes.

Place meat on grill and cook directly over hot coals, 4 to 5 minutes each side or until done. Serve as an appetizer with barbecue sauce or bleu cheese dressing.

Serves 15-18

Sausage-Stuffed Quail

6 whole quail
1/2 lb. pork sausage
6 T. finely chopped peanuts
salt and pepper to taste
red wine

Combine sausage and peanuts, and stuff quail. Salt and pepper birds to taste. Cook in a smoker at 250 degrees for 1 hour or until tender. Baste with red wine while cooking.

Serves 4-6

Cornish Hen à la Pepto

2 Cornish hens
4 T. cornstarch
4 T. sugar
1/2 t. salt
1 t. dry mustard
1/2 t. ground ginger
1 (1 lb.) can pitted sour red cherries
1/2 C. dry sherry
1-1/2 T. slivered orange peel
1/2 C. orange juice
1/4 C. red currant jelly

Grill hens for 1 hour (or until done) over medium hot coals, or bake in an oven at 425 degrees for 1 hour.

In a saucepan, combine cornstarch, sugar, salt, mustard, and ginger. Drain cherries and reserve the juice. Pour sherry over cherries and set aside. Add cherry juice to cornstarch mixture. Stir in orange peel, orange juice, and currant jelly. Cook over medium heat until mixture thickens. Add sherried cherries to mixture. Just before serving, pour over hens.

Serve with gourmet rice and broccoli or asparagus.

Serves 2

Marinated Duck Breasts

5 duck breasts, halved and deboned
thick bacon slices

MARINADE:

1/2 C. soy sauce
1/2 C. red wine
1 t. garlic salt
1 t. onion salt
2 C. zesty Italian dressing
1 t. Worcestershire sauce
1/2 t. meat tenderizer
1/4 t. garlic pepper
pinch of tarragon
pinch of rosemary

Combine marinade ingredients and marinate meat a minimum of 8 hours, turning often.

Remove breasts from liquid, wrap each in bacon, and brush with marinade. Char-grill as you would a small filet mignon (you may think that's what you're eating!).

Serves 8-10

Marinated Mallard Duck

2 ducks
1/4 C. cooking sherry

DRY MARINADE:

1 t. celery salt
1 t. onion salt
1 t. celery seed
1/2 t. curry powder
2 t. salt
1/2 t. black pepper

Place ducks in a pan, breast-side up, and drizzle with cooking sherry. Mix Dry Marinade and sprinkle over meat. Let stand in marinade 1 to 1-1/2 hours.

Place meat in a water-type smoker and cook at 250 degrees until tender.

Serves 4

FISH
AND SEAFOOD

Cajun Tuna

6 tuna fillets

MARINADE:

6 T. lemon juice
6 T. vegetable oil
2 T. Cajun Country Seasoning
2 t. lemon pepper

Combine marinade ingredients. Place fish in a glass dish with marinade for 2 hours, turning once.

Remove from marinade and grill over medium-hot coals for 5 to 8 minutes each side.

Serves 6

Lemon Grilled Orange Roughy

4 orange roughy fillets
1 stick butter, melted
juice of 1 lemon
1 clove garlic, minced
1 t. dill

    Mix butter, lemon juice, garlic, and dill. Baste fish with mixture. Grill over medium coals until fish flakes (about 15 minutes), basting frequently.

Serves 4

Grilled Salmon Steaks

2 salmon steaks
1/4 C. olive oil
1/4 C. pepper vinegar
1 clove garlic
1/2 t. salt
2 t. sugar

    Combine marinade ingredients and pour over salmon. Marinate in refrigerator for 1 to 2 hours.

    Grill salmon over medium-hot coals for 6 to 9 minutes per side.

Serves 2

Grilled Swordfish

1-3 lbs. swordfish
cooking oil spray

BASTING SAUCE:

1/2 lb. butter or margarine, melted
1 t. lemon pepper
1 t. garlic powder
2 T. lemon juice
1 T. Worcestershire sauce
2 t. parsley flakes
dash of hot sauce

Spray gas or charcoal grill with cooking oil. Heat gas grill to high, or let coals get hot if using charcoal.

Mix together Basting Sauce ingredients and baste both sides of fish. Sear fish to seal. Turn gas heat down to low or spread out charcoal. Cook on low heat for 45 minutes or until fish flakes with a fork. Baste throughout cooking process. Remove from fire and cut into serving pieces.

Serves 6

Big Ed's Barbecued Catfish Fillets

2 lbs. catfish fillets (1/2-in. thick)
6 oz. Allegro marinade

DRY SPICE MIX:

3 T. garlic powder
3 T. McCormick barbecue spice
1-1/2 T. celery salt
1 t. hickory-flavored salt

Marinate fillets for 30 minutes in Allegro marinade, then rub in a light covering of Dry Spice Mix. Place fish on charcoal-fired grill and cook over low heat until fillets becomes light and flaky.

Serves 6

Trout on the Grill

4 whole trout
1 stick butter
4 green onions, chopped
3 lemons
salt and pepper to taste

Melt butter in a saucepan, and add chopped onions and juice of 1 lemon. Thinly slice 1 lemon and place slices in cavities of each trout. Salt and pepper each fish inside and out. Brush on butter mixture, spooning some onions into the cavity of each trout.

Grill fish over hot coals for about 6 minutes on each side. Brush with marinade while cooking. Serve with wedges of lemon.

Serves 4

Prawns in Lemon Butter

2 lbs. large shrimp, peeled and deveined
1 C. melted butter
1/4 C. lemon juice
1 clove garlic, minced
1 t. parsley flakes
1 t. Worcestershire sauce
1 t. soy sauce
1/2 t. seasoned pepper
1/4 t. salt
1/4 t. garlic salt

Mix all ingredients except shrimp and bring to a boil. Thread shrimp onto water-soaked bamboo skewers and cook over medium-hot coals. Baste frequently with butter sauce until shrimp are opaque, 3 to 4 minutes per side.

Serves 4-6

Spiced Ginger Shrimp

2 lbs. shrimp, peeled and deveined

MARINADE:

2/3 C. soy sauce
1/2 C. olive oil
2 T. brown sugar
1-1/2 t. ground ginger
1 medium yellow onion, minced
2 cloves garlic, minced

Combine marinade ingredients and marinate shrimp overnight in the refrigerator.

Skewer shrimp and grill over direct charcoal heat for approximately 20 minutes.

Serves 4-6

RUBS, MARINADES, AND SAUCES

Dry Rub for Meats

1 T. lemon peel
1 T. garlic powder
1 T. onion powder
1 T. chili powder
1 T. paprika
1 T. MSG
1/2 T. black pepper
1/2 T. cayenne pepper
1/2 T. white pepper
2 T. salt
2 T. sugar

Combine all ingredients and rub into meat before cooking.

Savory Poultry Rub

1 T. garlic powder
2 T. tarragon
1 T. poultry seasoning
2 T. lemon pepper
1 T. paprika
2 t. salt

Combine all ingredients and rub into meat before cooking.

Sizzlers Dry Rub

2 T. paprika
1 T. onion salt
1 T. garlic salt
1 T. ground basil
1-1/2 T. lemon pepper
1 T. red pepper
1-1/2 T. black pepper
1 T. mustard flour (available at specialty grocers)

Combine all ingredients and rub into meat before cooking.

HST Sprinkle Spice

1 T. granulated garlic
1 T. onion powder
1 T. chili powder
1 T. paprika
1/2 T. lemon peel
1/2 T. orange peel
1/2 T. MSG (optional)
1/2 T. cayenne pepper

Combine all ingredients and mix well. Sprinkle on meat (ribs, shoulders, pork chops, chicken, steaks, brisket, fish, etc.) and let set for at least 1/2 hour before cooking.

David Cox's Dry Rub

5 T. paprika
4 T. MSG
2 t. garlic powder
2 t. cayenne pepper
1 t. white pepper
1 t. nutmeg
1 t. cloves
4 T. seasoned pepper
4 t. onion powder
3 T. chili powder
1 T. salt

Combine all ingredients and store in a tightly sealed glass jar. Rub liberally into meats before cooking.

Oriental Marinade

1 C. soy sauce
1/4 C. sesame oil
1/4 C. sugar
3 cloves garlic, minced
1 T. ground ginger
fresh ground pepper to taste

Combine all ingredients and blend well. This marinade is versatile—try it on salmon, pork tenderloin, and chicken breasts.

David Cox's Marinade

1 (6 oz.) can orange juice
1 (6 oz.) bottle lemon juice
1 C. vinegar
3/4 C. oil
1/4 C. water
1 T. Worcestershire sauce
1-1/2 t. salt
1 t. pepper
1 t. oregano
1/2 t. basil
1/4 t. garlic

Combine ingredients and use to marinate meats 2 hours to overnight (refrigerated) before cooking.

Basting Sauce

4 C. Wicker's Marinade and Baste
2 C. vegetable oil
2 C. apple cider vinegar (or unsweetened apple juice)
1/2 C. lemon juice

Combine all ingredients. Warm and use to baste meat every 45 minutes to 1 hour during cooking.

J-R's Basting Sauce

1 qt. apple cider vinegar
1 t. garlic powder
1 t. poultry seasoning
6 bay leaves
1 t. crushed red pepper
1 t. thyme
1 t. rosemary
1 t. lemon pepper

Mix all ingredients and bring to a rolling boil. Cover and let mixture cool completely. Use with any recipe that calls for a basting sauce.

Sizzlers Basting Sauce

1 qt. vinegar
1 pt. water
1/2 small can chili pepper
1 cup prepared mustard
1-1/4 C. brown sugar
1/2 stick butter
1/2 bottle root beer

Combine first four ingredients in a saucepan and mix well. Cook very slowly for 1 hour. Add brown sugar, butter, and root beer to mixture and slow boil for 30 minutes. Recommended for pork and wild game.

HST Basting Sauce

1 gal. apple cider vinegar
1 qt. Worcestershire sauce
1-1/4 C. lemon juice
3 heaping T. black pepper

Mix all ingredients in a large pot and bring to a hard boil for 10 minutes.

Wet Sauce

1 (10 oz.) bottle dark soy sauce
1 (46 oz.) can tomato juice
1 (10 oz.) bottle Worcestershire sauce
1 (24 oz.) bottle catsup
2 C. apple cider vinegar
2 C. brown sugar
juice of 2 lemons
2 t. red pepper
2 t. black pepper
2 t. dry mustard
1 t. garlic powder
1 t. onion powder
1 t. oregano
1 t. allspice
1 t. ginger
1 t. basil

Mix all ingredients in a saucepan and simmer for 1 hour. Let sauce stand for 2 hours before serving.

Horseradish Sauce for Beef

1/4 C. butter
1/4 C. flour
1 t. salt
1/4 t. pepper
2-1/4 C. milk
2 T. horseradish
1 T. A-1 Steak Sauce

Melt butter, stir in flour, and cook for 2 minutes, stirring constantly. Add other ingredients and cook until thickened.

Sizzlers
Barbecue Sauce

1 C. white vinegar
1 gal. barbecue sauce
1/2 C. prepared mustard
1 C. lemon juice
1 (12 oz.) can Coors beer
1 C. Worcestershire sauce
1 stick butter
2 C. paprika

Combine all ingredients in a saucepan. Bring to a boil and simmer mixture for 1 hour. (If a sweeter taste is desired, add brown sugar; if a hot taste is preferable, add red pepper.)

Vinegar-Based Barbecue Sauce

1 (1-1/4 oz.) can black pepper
1 (1-1/4 oz.) can red pepper
2 qts. white vinegar
2 T. sugar
1/2 C. salt
1/4 C. lemon juice
1 small bottle catsup

Boil first six ingredients for 8 minutes, then add catsup. Boil for 2 more minutes.

Coke Barbecue Sauce

2 C. Coca-Cola
2 C. catsup
2 C. white vinegar
1-1/2 T. black pepper
3 T. chili powder
3 T. salt
3 T. sugar
1/2 large onion, chopped fine

Mix all ingredients in a saucepan and bring to a boil. Reduce heat and cook slowly for 1 to 2 hours, stirring occasionally.

HST Serving Sauce

1/2 stick butter
1/3 C. lemon juice
1/4 C. soy sauce
1/4 C. Louisiana hot sauce
2 t. dry mustard
1-1/2 t. garlic powder
1 t. basil
1 t. red pepper
1 t. chili powder
1 t. ginger
1/2 C. brown sugar
1/3 C. white vinegar
1/4 C. Worcestershire sauce
3 dashes Tabasco sauce
1-1/2 t. onion powder
1 t. allspice
1 t. black pepper
1 t. celery seed
1 t. dill
1 t. oregano
1 (18 oz.) bottle tomato-based barbecue sauce (plain)

   Melt butter in a medium saucepan over low heat. Add liquid ingredients next, and then stir in remaining ingredients one at a time. Add commercial barbecue sauce last. Simmer for 30 minutes, stirring often. Age at least 2 days in the refrigerator.

★ ★

SIDE DISHES

★ ★

Smoker-Cooked Beans

7 (1 lb.) cans pork and beans
1 C. chopped onion
3/4 C. chopped bell pepper
2-1/2 C. catsup
3/4 C. Worcestershire sauce
3/4 C. brown sugar
3/4 C. honey
1 lb. bacon, diced and partially cooked

Mix all ingredients well and pour into a disposable aluminum pan. Keep temperature around 275 degrees and cook beans uncovered on hot end of smoker 3 to 4 hours or until liquid is cooked down.

Serves 20-25

Dee's Crooked Neck Squash

4 medium yellow crookneck squash, sliced
salt and pepper to taste

Layer sliced squash on heavy-duty aluminum foil, sprinkling salt and pepper between layers. Tightly close foil and place in a disposable aluminum pan. Cook over medium-hot fire for 20 to 30 minutes.

Serves 6-8

Rosemary and Garlic
Sweet Potatoes

4 lbs. sweet potatoes
1/2 C. olive oil
1-1/2 T. dried rosemary, crumbled
24 unpeeled garlic cloves, flattened
freshly ground pepper to taste

Peel and cut sweet potatoes into 1/3- to 1/2-inch rounds. Combine with other ingredients (season generously with pepper) and divide mixture into two large baking dishes (or disposable aluminum pans). Stir to coat sweet potatoes.

Grill over medium fire (or bake in a 450-degree oven) about 50 minutes or until potatoes are tender and crusty. Stir occasionally while cooking.

Serves 12

Custer's Eola Hotel Pickled Vidalia Onions

3 Vidalia or white onions, peeled and sliced

MARINADE:

1/2 C. sugar
1/2 C. white vinegar
1 C. vegetable oil
1 t. dry mustard
1/2 t. red pepper
salt to taste

To prepare the marinade, dissolve sugar in vinegar, then add oil, followed by spices. Add peeled and sliced onions, separated into rings (be sure you have enough liquid to cover the onions). Let marinate 12 to 24 hours. Serve as a side dish with any barbecue.

Make more than you think you'll need—they're eaten quickly and you'll wish you had more!

Serves 6-8

Grilled Corn on the Cob

6-8 fresh yellow or white corn in husks
butter
salt and pepper

Pull husks down 3 or 4 inches and remove corn silks. Soak corn in iced water for 30 to 45 minutes.

Replace husks and place ears on grill. Cook for about 45 minutes or until done. Remove from grill. Husks may be peeled back to form a "handle" or discarded. Butter and sprinkle with salt and pepper to taste.

Serves 4-6

Veggie Kabob

2 red bell peppers, quartered
2 green bell peppers, quartered
2 yellow squash, sliced 1-in. thick
1 onion, quartered
olive oil
salt and lemon pepper to taste

Thread vegetables onto skewers, alternating colors attractively. Drizzle with olive oil and season to taste with salt and lemon pepper. Grill over hot coals for 5 minutes, turning often, then move to opposite side of grill and cook covered for an additional 10 minutes.

Serves 4

Grilled Tomatoes

6 medium, firm tomatoes
1/2 t. seasoned salt
1/2 t. seasoned pepper
1/2 C. seasoned bread crumbs (Italian)
1/4 cup Parmesan cheese
1/3 cup Russian or Catalina dressing
dash of hot sauce (to taste)
fresh parsley sprigs

Wash tomatoes. For each, using a V-shape garnishing tool or sharp knife, make a zigzag cut beginning at stem end. Proceed all around tomato. Remove top section and hollow out tomato to make a shell. Save tomato pulp in a mixing bowl. Drain off some excess juice from pulp and discard. Add salt, pepper, bread crumbs, cheese, salad dressing, and hot sauce (mixture should be medium thick but not soupy). Return mixture to tomatoes.

Grill until still firm (don't overcook), 5 to 10 minutes depending on temperature of grill. Garnish with parsley sprigs before serving.

To vary the stuffing, add chopped Vidalia onions and/or grated cheddar cheese.

Serves 4-6

MAIL ORDER SOURCES

Cajun Country Seasoning is the family recipe barbecue spice used so successfully by the Cajun Country Cookers, a champion team of barbecuers. Cajun Country Cookers also markets Cajun Country Rice. Write: Cajun Country Cookers, P.O. Box 3201, Jackson, TN 38303.

Rendezvous. The Rendezvous has been a favorite Memphis eatery since 1948 and now ships ribs, sauce, and Mr. Charlie's famous seasoning by mail and Federal Express. Write: The Rendezvous, 52 S. Second St., Memphis TN 38103, or call (901) 523-2746.

Wicker Barbecue Products, a blend of vinegar and spices, are favored by certain barbecue teams but sometimes hard to find. The product line includes low-sodium varieties. Write: Wicker Barbecue Products, P.O. Box 126, Hornersville, MO 63855, or call (800) 847-0032 (in Missouri, (314) 737-2372).

Willingham's. John Willingham sells his W'ham cookers, sauces, seasonings, and barbecue meats by mail and Federal Express. Write: John Willingham, Willingham's World Champion BBQ, 6189 Heather Dr., Memphis, TN 38119, or call (800) 527-2683 (in Tennessee, (901) 362-RIBS).

★ ★ ★ ★ MAIL ORDER SOURCES ★ ★ ★ ★

Several giftshops specialize in Memphis products and barbecue products in particular. Write or call for descriptions
or catalogs of their offerings:

THE SHOPS OF ANN ADLER
A Basket Case
4966 Poplar Avenue
Memphis, TN 38117
(901) 683-1700
3116 Village Shops
Germantown, TN 38138
(901) 753-5453

BASQUETTES
5101 Sanderlin Centre
#114
Memphis, TN 38117
(901) 763-4893

CENTER FOR SOUTHERN FOLKLORE
152 Beale Street
Memphis, TN 38111
(901) 525-3655

DELECTABLES LTD.
4741 Poplar Avenue
Memphis, TN 38117
(901) 767-1987

HUNTER BASQUETRIE, INC.
376 Perkins Road Extended
Memphis, TN 38117
(901) 761-1988

PEABODY GIFTSHOP
149 Union
Memphis, TN 38103
(901) 526-3825

PINK PALACE MUSEUM GIFTSHOP
3050 Central Ave.
Memphis, TN 38111
(901) 320-6401

ABOUT THE AUTHOR

Carolyn Wells is hog wild for barbecue. She cut her teeth on rib bones and blossomed on plenty of backyard barbecues, church "socials," and pig sandwiches from local barbecue joints in her native Nashville.

By adulthood she definitely had basting sauce in her veins. She even pursued a career in 'Que. For 13 years she was affiliated with Wicker Barbecue Products Company in Hornersville, Missouri, about 80 miles from Memphis. Through this association, she became acquainted with (and addicted to) Memphis-style barbecue, sampling it at the great Memphis barbecue restaurants and at the barbecue contests she attended. She even began entering the contests herself and to date has won over 50 trophies and ribbons in various competitions. In 1987, she left Wicker's and started a barbecue-related marketing and consulting business.

Carolyn, who also authored *Barbecue Greats Memphis Style: Great Restaurants, Great Recipes, Great Personalities*, lives now with her husband Gary and family in the Kansas City area.

ORDER FORM

Order direct—Call 800-877-3119

I want to cook like a pro. Please send me:

_____copy(s) of **All About Bar-B-Q Kansas City Style** for $14.95

_____copy(s) of **Barbecue Greats Memphis Style** for $14.95

_____copy(s) of **Texas Barbecue** for $14.95

_____Please send your **FREE CATALOG**

Shipping and handling: Please add as follows:

1 book—$3.75; 2 books—$4.75; 3-5 books—$6.00

Method of Payment

_____Enclosed is my check for $_____
(payable to PIG OUT PUBLICATIONS, INC.)

Please charge to my credit card:_____VISA _____MasterCard

Acct.#_____Exp. Date_____

Signature_____

Ship to: **Gift/Ship to:**

_____   _____

_____   _____

_____   _____

_____   **From** _____

Mail completed order form to:

Pig Out Publications • 4245 Walnut • Kansas City, MO 64111